Children in our World

Refugees and Migrants

Ceri Roberts

Hanane Kai

Leabharlanna Poibli Chathair Baile Átha Cliath

Dublin City Public Libraries

WAYLAND

www.waylandbooks.co.uk

Published in Great Britain in 2018 by Wayland

Text © Wayland, 2016
Written by Ceri Roberts
Illustrations © Hanane Kai, 2016

Texturing of illustrations by Sarah Habli
Additional illustration work by Ashley Choukeir
Edited by Corinne Lucas
Designed by Sophie Wilkins

A catalogue for this title is available from the British Library.
ISBN: 978 1 5263 0021 8
10 9 8 7 6 5 4 3 2 1

MIX
Paper from
responsible sources
FSC
www.fsc.org   FSC® C104740

Printed in China

Wayland
An imprint of
Hachette Children's Books
Part of Hodder & Stoughton
Carmelite House
50 Victoria Embankment
London, EC4Y 0DZ

An Hachette UK Company
www.hachette.co.uk
www.hachettechildrens.co.uk

Contents

Our home is the place where we spend time with the people we love, eat our favourite food, play with toys, and sleep in a warm bed.

Sometimes people leave their home because war, a natural disaster or terrorism mean that it's dangerous to stay. These people are known as refugees. Others leave for a happier, healthier life, to join family members overseas, or because they don't have enough money and need a job. People who choose to do this are called migrants.

Not all migrants leave home because they are living in poverty, but this book will look at the different reasons why people need to escape to other countries, and what happens to them afterwards.

Some refugees and migrants are children who travel with a parent or guardian, but every year tens of thousands of children make long journeys without a grown-up. This is usually because they are orphans, or they were separated from their parents on the way.

If you've ever lost your mum or dad for a few minutes at the park or shop, you know how scary it feels when you're by yourself. It's much harder for children who are alone in a strange country. They often don't speak the language or have anywhere to sleep, and they miss their family and friends.

Refugees and migrants travel from countries all over the world. Some flee because of terrorism and war. Others leave because their lives are at risk because of who they are or what they believe.

Often refugees and migrants come from developing countries where people don't live long lives, have much money, and many children don't go to school. Sometimes their homes have been destroyed by natural disasters, such as a hurricane, earthquake or flood.

If you've ever moved house you'll know it's normal to pack
up your belongings and take them with you. When you
go on holiday, you fill a suitcase with your clothes
and toys. Refugees usually leave their homes
in a hurry so they don't have time to pack.
Even if they do, they can't carry heavy bags
over long distances. Some manage to take
a small bag with them, but this can get
lost along the way. Most have nothing
left to remind them of home.

Many refugees and migrants don't have a passport and visa, which are the documents you need to get in to another country. This means they aren't allowed to travel by plane so their journey can take weeks, or even months.

Refugees and migrants are often so desperate that they risk their life and pay smugglers to transport them to another country. Some spend days hidden in a lorry without food or water. They have to keep very quiet and are scared that they might be found.

Others travel across rough seas in overcrowded boats. Many more walk for weeks in extreme weather conditions, without warm clothes, waterproofs, or anywhere to sleep. Sadly, some don't survive the dangerous journey. It's important that we find ways to help so that they won't have to put themselves in danger.

Refugees and migrants want to live in a country where they feel safe.

Just like everyone else, they dream of a warm, comfortable home, to take care of their family, get a job or go to school. Only then will they be able to do the everyday things that we take for granted, such as buying their favourite foods, watching television and having fun with friends.

15

By the time they reach their destination, most refugees and migrants have only the clothes they are wearing. Usually, they have no money or anywhere to stay. It's hard to get help when they don't know who to ask, or speak the country's language.

This is why many refugees and migrants end up homeless, or living in tents, caravans or shacks in refugee camps. Although this isn't as comfortable as living in a proper house, there are lots of helpers who hand out food, clothing and medicine to people.

If you've been camping, you probably had lots of fun, but life in refugee camps is very hard. Families have to live together in small spaces, and children don't have their own room, or even their own bed. Some don't have a bed at all.

In some places, it's very hot in the summer and very cold in the winter. There's no electricity or running water, so it's difficult to keep clean. People have to queue for hours for food or medicine, and there are no proper schools.

Refugee camps are home to thousands of people, and some families live there for many years. This is why doctors, nurses, teachers and other volunteers go and help people settle in, build communities and schools, and stay healthy.

Teams of volunteers from charities and government organisations work hard to help people who are living in refugee camps. Some doctors and nurses set up clinics where they can treat people who are ill. Other volunteers help to build shelters, or set up schools for children. Many more people help by collecting clothes or food.

When a refugee or migrant arrives in a new country they have to ask the government for permission to stay. This is called 'seeking asylum' and it can be very complicated and confusing.

Governments help asylum seekers find a place to live and give them a small amount of money for food and other things they need. Asylum seeks who are children, travelling without an adult, usually live in children's homes or with foster families, who keep them safe.

Not all asylum seekers are allowed to stay in a country, so they might ask the government to think again, seek asylum in another country, or live in refugee camps. Some are sent back to their home country.

When asylum is given, people gain official refugee status. This means that they can stay in their new country for a number of years. During this time they can work to earn money and create a better life for their family. Children can go to school, where they make new friends and sometimes learn a new language. So if you meet a new child at school from another country, it's important to make them feel welcome.

If, after a period of time, it's still not safe for refugees to return to their home country, they can apply to stay forever. This means that they won't have to worry about the future, and can enjoy a safe and happy life in their new home.

BRAINSE DOMHNACH MIDE
DONAGHMEDE BRANCH
TEL: 8482833

25

It's good to care about other people, but it can be upsetting to think about what life is like for refugees and migrants. If you are sad or worried, it is important to talk to an adult about how you feel. Together, you can think about ways that you can help.

Remember, most people have a safe and comfortable home to live in. You and your family are not at great risk of becoming refugees or migrants. There are lots of clever people working hard to stop wars and terrorism, and end poverty all around the world. They want to make sure that everyone can live happily.

Lots of people are already helping refugees and migrants, but there are many ways that you can help, too. You could collect food, clothes, toys or books to send to refugee camps. You could organise a bake sale or take part in a sponsored challenge to raise money for charities that help refugees. You could even write a letter to the government asking them to do more to look after people in need.

Find Out More

Books

Azzi In Between
Sarah Garland, Frances Lincoln Children's Books, 2015

Juliane's Story — A Journey from Zimbabwe (Seeking Refuge),
Andy Glynne, Wayland, 2016

Who are Refugees and Migrants? What Makes People Leave their Homes? And Other Big Questions.
Michael Rosen and Annemarie Young, Wayland, 2016

Websites

Care International helps refugees all over the world.
www.careinternational.org.uk

Refugee Action helps refugees to build new lives in the UK.
www.refugee-action.org.uk

Unicef helps to protect children who are in danger.
www.unicef.org.uk

Save the Children works to protect children in need all over the world.
www.savethechildren.org.uk

The Red Cross is a charity that helps victims of war and disaster.
www.redcross.org.uk

Glossary

asylum protection given by a country to a person who has left their home country as a refugee

charity group that helps those in need

developing countries places in the world where people don't live long lives, have much money or always go to school

foster family people who take care of children when their parents can't

government group of people who control and make decisions for a country

migrant person who leaves their home country to find a better life

natural disaster natural events that cause great damage, such as a hurricane, flood or earthquake

orphan child whose mother and father have both died

refugee a person who leaves their home country to find a safer place to live

refugee camp a place where refugees can stay when they have escaped their home country

smugglers people who secretly take things, or other people, to a different place

terrorism using violent acts to scare people and make them do what you want

volunteer someone who gives up their time to help other people without being paid

war when people fight against each other

Marino Branch
Brainse Marino
Tel: 8336297

Index